THE PEACEFUL

Word

CATHY DUPLANTIS

The Peaceful Word
ISBN 978-1-941190-65-4
Copyright © 2014 Cathy Duplantis
Published by Jesse Duplantis Ministries
First Printing 2014

Jesse Duplantis Ministries
PO Box 1089
Destrehan, LA 70047
USA
www.jdm.org

Jesse Duplantis Ministries is dedicated to reaching people and changing lives with the Gospel of Jesus Christ. For more information or to purchase other products from Jesse Duplantis Ministries, please contact us at the address above.

*This book is lovingly dedicated
to my husband, Jesse.*

"I am leaving you with a gift—peace of mind and heart. And the peace I give is a gift the world cannot give. So don't be troubled or afraid." ~Jesus Christ
(John 14:27 NLT)

The Gift of Peace

Many hundreds of years before the birth of Jesus, Isaiah 9:6 declared the great plan of God to bring peace on earth. *"For unto us a Child is born, unto us a Son is given: and the government shall be upon His shoulder: and His name shall be called Wonderful, Counsellor, The Mighty God, The Everlasting Father, The Prince of Peace."*

Peace is defined as, "a state of tranquility or quiet; a pact or agreement to end hostilities between those who have been at war or in a state of enmity; harmony in personal relations, especially with God; a state of security or order within a community; freedom from disquieting or oppressive thoughts or emotions."

God wants everyone on the earth to experience true peace. He sent an angel to proclaim the birth of His Son to bring peace on earth. Once the news was announced to the shepherds watching their flock in the night, Luke 2:13-14 says, *"And suddenly there was with the angel a multitude of the heavenly host praising God, and saying, Glory to God in the highest, and on earth peace, good will toward men."*

On earth PEACE! This was a declaration that served notice on the devil that his days of tormenting God's creation were numbered. God thought of a great plan to restore mankind by sending His Son to die on the cross for the sins of the world.

This gift of peace must be received by faith, so don't try to "feel" it. Believe it! Ephesians 2:14-18 tells us, *"For He is our peace, Who hath made both one, and hath broken down the middle wall of partition between us; Having abolished in His flesh the enmity, even the law of commandments contained in ordinances; for to make in Himself of twain one new man, so making peace; And that He might reconcile both unto God in one body by the cross, having slain the enmity thereby: And came and preached peace to you which were afar off, and to them that were nigh. For through Him we both have access by one Spirit unto the Father."*

A Gift the World Cannot Give

Years ago I saw a simple, yet very powerful statement on a sign in front of a small church that I have never forgotten. It said, "Know God, Know Peace. No God, No Peace."

That is really true. This great gift of peace is a God thing that the world cannot give. During the last supper with His disciples, Jesus said, *"I am leaving you with a gift— peace of mind and heart. And the peace I give is a gift the world cannot give. So don't be troubled or afraid"* (John 14:27 NLT).

This life-changing message of peace by Jesus Christ must be preached to the world. Acts 10:36-38 says, *"The Word which God sent unto the children of Israel, preaching peace by Jesus Christ: (He is Lord of all:) That Word, I say, ye know, which was published throughout all Judaea, and began from Galilee, after the baptism which John preached; How God anointed Jesus of Nazareth with the Holy Ghost and with power: Who went about doing good, and healing all that were oppressed of the devil; for God was with Him."*

Jesus came to destroy the works of the devil and deliver us from every form of darkness. In John 16:33 (AMP), He promised us, *"I have told you these things, so that in Me you may have [perfect] peace and confidence. In the world you have tribulation and trials and distress and frustration; but be of good cheer [take courage; be confident, certain, undaunted]! For I have overcome the world. [I have deprived it of power to harm you and have conquered it for you.]"*

Realize today that Jesus has come to give you perfect peace and confidence. You don't have to be distressed or frustrated by the problems in the world. Philippians 4:6-9 says, *"Be careful for nothing; but in every thing by prayer and supplication with thanksgiving let your requests be made known unto God. And the peace of God, which passeth all understanding, shall keep your hearts and minds through Christ Jesus. Finally, brethren, whatsoever things are true, whatsoever things are honest, whatsoever things are just, whatsoever things are pure, whatsoever things are lovely, whatsoever things are of good report; if there be any virtue, and if there be any praise, think on these things. Those things, which ye have both learned, and received, and heard, and seen in me, do: and the God of peace shall be with you."*

You are in the world, but it doesn't need to bring distress to your life. You have God's promise that you can pray about everything and allow the peace of God to keep your heart and mind through Christ Jesus. You can decide to think on things in God's Word that are true, honest, just, pure, lovely, of good report and virtue, and stay full of praise. God's amazing gift of peace is available for you—every moment of every day. As you read and meditate on the four steps and scriptures in *The Peaceful Word*, accept God's gift of peace and allow Him to fill you with courage to change your world. Great gifts always do that!

Step One

Realize That God's
Gift Of Peace Is
Yours Today

John 14:27 **Peace** *I leave with you, My* **peace** *I give unto you: not as the world giveth, give I unto you. Let not your heart be troubled, neither let it be afraid.*

John 14:27 **Peace** *I leave with you;* **My [own] peace** *I now give and bequeath to you. Not as the world gives do I give to you. Do not let your hearts be troubled, neither let them be afraid. [Stop allowing yourselves to be agitated and disturbed; and do not permit yourselves to be fearful and intimidated and cowardly and unsettled] (AMP).*

John 14:27 *I'm leaving you well and whole. That's My parting gift to you.* **Peace.** *I don't leave you the way you're used to being left—feeling abandoned, bereft. So don't be upset. Don't be distraught (MSG).*

14

2 Thessalonians 3:16 *Now* **the Lord of peace** *Himself* **give you peace always** *by all means. The Lord be with you all.*

Luke 1:76–79 *And thou, child, shalt be called the prophet of the Highest: for thou shalt go before the face of the Lord to prepare His ways;*

To give knowledge of salvation unto His people by the remission of their sins,

Through the tender mercy of our God; whereby the Dayspring from on high hath visited us,

To give light to them that sit in darkness and in the shadow of death, ***to guide our feet into the way of peace***.

Luke 2:14 *Glory to God in the highest, and* **on earth peace**, *good will toward men.*

James 3:17-18 *But the wisdom that is from above is first pure, then* **peaceable**, *gentle, and easy to be intreated, full of mercy and good fruits, without partiality, and without hypocrisy.*

And the fruit of righteousness is sown in **peace** *of them that make* **peace**.

Psalm 55:18 *He has **redeemed my life in peace** from the battle that was against me [so that none came near me], for they were many who strove with me (AMP).*

Isaiah 50:4-5 *The Lord G*OD *hath given me the tongue of the learned, that I should know how to speak a word in season to him that is weary: He wakeneth morning by morning, He wakeneth mine ear to hear as the learned.*

*The Lord G*OD *hath opened mine ear, and I was not rebellious, neither turned away back.*

Jeremiah 29:11 *For I know the thoughts that I think toward you, saith the L*ORD*, **thoughts of peace**, and not of evil, to give you an expected end.*

Isaiah 53:4–5 *Surely He hath borne our griefs, and carried our sorrows: yet we did esteem Him stricken, smitten of God, and afflicted.*

But He was wounded for our transgressions, He was bruised for our iniquities: the chastisement of **our peace was upon Him***; and with His stripes we are healed.*

1 Corinthians 14:33 For God is not the author of confusion, but of **peace**, as in all churches of the saints.

Romans 15:13 *Now the God of hope **fill you with all joy and peace in believing**, that ye may abound in hope, through the power of the Holy Ghost.*

Step Two

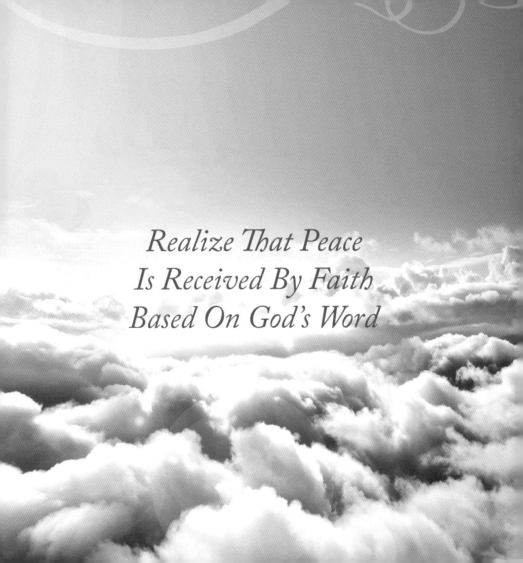

*Realize That Peace
Is Received By Faith
Based On God's Word*

Psalm 55:22 *Cast your burden on the Lord [releasing the weight of it] and He will sustain you; He will never allow the [consistently] righteous to be moved (made to slip, fall, or fail) (AMP).*

Philippians 4:6–9 *Be careful for nothing; but in every thing by prayer and supplication with thanksgiving let your requests be made known unto God.*

*And the **peace of God**, which passeth all understanding, shall keep your hearts and minds through Christ Jesus.*

Finally, brethren, whatsoever things are true, whatsoever things are honest, whatsoever things are just, whatsoever things are pure, whatsoever things are lovely, whatsoever things are of good report; if there be any virtue, and if there be any praise, think on these things.

*Those things, which ye have both learned, and received, and heard, and seen in me, do: and the **God of peace** shall be with you.*

John 16:33 *I have told you these things, so that in Me* **you may have [perfect] peace** *and confidence. In the world you have tribulation and trials and distress and frustration; but be of good cheer [***take courage; be confident***, certain, undaunted]! For I have overcome the world.* **[I have deprived it of power to harm you** *and have conquered it for you] (AMP).*

Romans 5:1-2 *Therefore, since we have been made right in God's sight by faith,* **we have peace** *with God because of what Jesus Christ our Lord has done for us.*

Because of our faith, Christ has brought us into this place of undeserved privilege where we now stand, and we confidently and joyfully look forward to sharing God's glory (NLT).

Ephesians 4:1-3 *I therefore, the prisoner of the Lord, beseech you that ye walk worthy of the vocation wherewith ye are called,*

With all lowliness and meekness, with longsuffering, forbearing one another in love;

Endeavouring to keep the unity of the Spirit in the bond of peace.

Ephesians 6:10-18 *Finally, my brethren, be strong in the Lord, and in the power of His might.*

Put on the whole armour of God, that ye may be able to stand against the wiles of the devil.

For we wrestle not against flesh and blood, but against principalities, against powers, against the rulers of the darkness of this world, against spiritual wickedness in high places.

Wherefore take unto you the whole armour of God, that ye may be able to withstand in the evil day, and having done all, to stand.

Stand therefore, having your loins girt about with truth, and having on the breastplate of righteousness;

*And your feet shod with the preparation of the **Gospel of peace**;*

*Above all, **taking the shield of faith**, wherewith ye shall be able to quench all the fiery darts of the wicked.*

And take the helmet of salvation, and the sword of the Spirit, which is the Word of God:

Praying always with all prayer and supplication in the Spirit, and watching thereunto with all perseverance and supplication for all saints.

Galatians 5:22–23 *But the fruit of the Spirit is love, joy, **peace**, longsuffering, gentleness, goodness, faith, Meekness, temperance: against such there is no law.*

Step Three

*Realize That You
Have A Right To A
Peaceful Life*

Ephesians 2:14–18 *For **He is our peace**, Who hath made both one, and hath broken down the middle wall of partition between us;*

*Having abolished in His flesh the enmity, even the law of commandments contained in ordinances; for to make in Himself of twain one new man, so making **peace**;*

And that He might reconcile both unto God in one body by the cross, having slain the enmity thereby:

*And came and preached **peace to you** which were afar off, and to them that were nigh.*

For through Him we both have access by one Spirit unto the Father.

Acts 10:36–38 *The Word which God sent unto the children of Israel, preaching **peace** by Jesus Christ: (He is Lord of all:)*

That Word, I say, ye know, which was published throughout all Judaea, and began from Galilee, after the baptism which John preached;

How God anointed Jesus of Nazareth with the Holy Ghost and with power: Who went about doing good, and healing all that were oppressed of the devil; for God was with Him.

Hebrews 13:20-21 *Now the God of **peace**, that brought again from the dead our Lord Jesus, that great Shepherd of the sheep, through the blood of the everlasting covenant,*

Make you perfect in every good work to do His will, working in you that which is wellpleasing in His sight, through Jesus Christ; to Whom be glory for ever and ever. Amen.

2 Peter 1:2–4 *Grace and **peace** be multiplied unto you through the knowledge of God, and of Jesus our Lord,*

According as His divine power hath given unto us all things that pertain unto life and godliness, through the knowledge of Him that hath called us to glory and virtue:

Whereby are given unto us exceeding great and precious promises: that by these ye might be partakers of the divine nature, having escaped the corruption that is in the world through lust.

Isaiah 54:13–17 *And all thy children shall be taught of the* L<small>ORD</small>; *and great shall be the* **peace** *of thy children.*

In righteousness shalt thou be established: thou shalt be far from oppression; for thou shalt not fear: and from terror; for it shall not come near thee.

Behold, they shall surely gather together, but not by Me: whosoever shall gather together against thee shall fall for thy sake.

Behold, I have created the smith that bloweth the coals in the fire, and that bringeth forth an instrument for his work; and I have created the waster to destroy.

No weapon that is formed against thee shall prosper; and every tongue that shall rise against thee in judgment thou shalt condemn. This is the heritage of the servants of the L<small>ORD</small>, *and their righteousness is of Me, saith the* L<small>ORD</small>.

Exodus 14:14 *The L*ORD *shall fight for you, and ye shall hold your* **peace***.*

Proverbs 16:7 *When a man's ways please the Lord, He makes even his enemies to be at* **peace** *with him (AMP).*

Colossians 1:19–20 For God in all His fullness was pleased to live in Christ, and through Him God reconciled everything to Himself. He made **peace** with everything in Heaven and on earth by means of Christ's blood on the cross (NLT).

Psalm 56:3-4 *But when I am afraid, I will put my trust in You. I praise God for what He has promised. I trust in God, so why should I be afraid? What can mere mortals do to me? (NLT)*

Proverbs 1:33 *But all who listen to Me will live in **peace**, untroubled by fear of harm (NLT).*

Psalm 85:8 *I will listen [with expectancy] to what God the Lord will say, for He will speak* **peace** *to His people, to His saints (those who are in right standing with Him)—but let them not turn again to [self-confident] folly (AMP).*

Psalm 29:11 *The* L*ord* *gives His people strength. The* L*ord* *blesses them with* **peace** *(NLT).*

Psalm 35:27 *But give great joy to those who came to my defense. Let them continually say, "Great is the L*ORD*, Who delights in blessing His servant with* **peace***!" (NLT)*

Psalm 119:165 *Those who love Your instructions have great **peace** and do not stumble (NLT).*

*Isaiah 26:3-4 You will guard him and keep him in **perfect and constant peace** whose mind [both its inclination and its character] is stayed on You, because he commits himself to You, leans on You, and hopes confidently in You.*

So trust in the Lord (commit yourself to Him, lean on Him, hope confidently in Him) forever; for the Lord God is an everlasting Rock [the Rock of Ages] (AMP).

Psalm 23 The LORD is my shepherd; I have all that I need.

He lets me rest in green meadows; He leads me beside **peaceful** streams.

He renews my strength. He guides me along right paths, bringing honor to His name.

Even when I walk through the darkest valley, I will not be afraid, for You are close beside me. Your rod and Your staff protect and comfort me.

You prepare a feast for me in the presence of my enemies. You honor me by anointing my head with oil. My cup overflows with blessings.

Surely Your goodness and unfailing love will pursue me all the days of my life, and I will live in the house of the LORD forever (NLT).

Genesis 15:15 *And thou shalt go to thy fathers in **peace**; thou shalt be buried in a good old age.*

Psalm 4:8 *In **peace** I will both lie down and sleep, for You, Lord, alone make me dwell in safety and confident trust (AMP).*

2 Corinthians 13:11 *Finally, brethren, farewell. Be perfect, be of good comfort, be of one mind, live in **peace**; and the God of love and **peace** shall be with you.*

Step Four

*Express Your
Thankfulness To God
For His Peaceful Word*

Colossians 3:15–17 *And let the **peace** that comes from Christ rule in your hearts. For as members of one body you are called to **live in peace**. And always **be thankful**.*

*Let the message about Christ, in all its richness, fill your lives. Teach and counsel each other with all the wisdom He gives. Sing psalms and hymns and spiritual songs to God with **thankful** hearts.*

*And whatever you do or say, do it as a representative of the Lord Jesus, **giving thanks** through Him to God the Father (NLT).*

1 Corinthians 15:57 But **thanks** be to God, which giveth us the victory through our Lord Jesus Christ.

1 Chronicles 16:8 Give **thanks** to the L*ORD* and proclaim His greatness. Let the whole world know what He has done (NLT).

Psalm 30:11-12 You have turned my mourning into joyful dancing. You have taken away my clothes of mourning and clothed me with joy, that I might sing praises to you and not be silent. O L*ORD* my God, I will give You **thanks** forever! (NLT)

Psalm 107:1-2 O give **thanks** unto the L ORD, for He is good: for His mercy endureth for ever.

Let the redeemed of the L ORD say so, whom He hath redeemed from the hand of the enemy.

Psalms 140:13 Surely the righteous shall give **thanks** unto Thy name: the upright shall dwell in Thy presence.

2 Corinthians 2:14 Now **thanks** be unto God, which always causeth us to triumph in Christ, and maketh manifest the savour of His knowledge by us in every place.

Hebrews 13:15 By Him therefore let us offer the sacrifice of praise to God continually, that is, the fruit of our lips giving **thanks** to His name.

Take Courage

If something in your life is causing you distress by robbing you of God's gift of peace, you can do something today that will begin to turn it around. Whether it is fear, sickness, persecution, or any distressing situation that comes against you or the ones you love, you don't have to shrink back in fear. You can overcome and change that seemingly hopeless situation.

How can you do that? By taking courage!

The Amplified Bible translation of Psalm 31:24 says, *"Be strong and let your heart take courage, all you who wait for and hope for and expect the Lord!"*

Courage has been defined as mental and moral strength. It is a force that empowers us to rise above the distress and troubles in life with **perfect peace** that is beyond human understanding. Courage made a shepherd boy sling a rock at a giant and win the battle for his nation. This same force of courage can enable you to live in **perfect peace** every day of your life.

1 Chronicles 28:20 says that, *"David said to Solomon his son, Be strong and of good courage, and do it: fear not, nor be dismayed: for the L*ord *God, even my God, will be with thee; He will not fail thee, nor forsake thee, until thou hast finished all the work for the service of the house of the L*ord.*"*

That, too, was Jesus' answer to the distressing situations His disciples would face while they were in the world. He said, *"I have told you these things, so that in Me you may have [perfect] peace and confidence. In the world you have tribulation and trials and distress and frustration; but be of good cheer [take courage; be confident, certain, undaunted]! For I have overcome the world. [I have deprived it of power to harm you and have conquered it for you]"* (John 16:33 AMP).

The word "cheer" in *Vines Expository Dictionary of New Testament Words* signifies being "put in good spirits" and being "of good courage." It can also be expressed as meaning "confidence" or being "merry." So being cheerful is essential for building a victorious and peaceful life.

The storm that attacked the ship carrying the Apostle Paul to Caesar had distressed those on board until all hope of being saved was lost. But Paul never gave up hope. He was an expert at turning a distressing situation into a victory celebration. Acts chapter 27 gives us the account of the events:

And when neither sun nor stars were visible for many days and no small tempest kept raging about us, all hope of our being saved was finally abandoned.

Then as they had eaten nothing for a long time, Paul came forward into their midst and said, Men, you should have listened to me, and should not have put to sea from Crete and brought on this disaster and harm and misery and loss.

But [even] now I beg you to be in good spirits and take heart, for there will be no loss of life among you but only of the ship.

For this [very] night there stood by my side an angel of the God to Whom I belong and Whom I serve and worship,

And he said, Do not be frightened, Paul! It is necessary for you to stand before Caesar; and behold, God has given you all those who are sailing with you.

So keep up your courage, men, for I have faith (complete confidence) in God that it will be exactly as it was told me;

Acts 27:20-25 AMP

We know from the rest of the story that Paul and all that sailed with him that day were saved. This amazing testimony of faith in God's Word was recorded by the Holy Spirit in order to inspire each of us to keep up our courage anytime we face a distressing situation. Belief in God's Word releases supernatural power to quiet the storms of life and bring **lasting peace** to a troubled heart.

We have so many examples of wonderful men and women of God that overcame distressing situations because they refused to walk in fear and were determined to take courage. Daniel, Esther, and Jeremiah, just to name a few, could never have walked in victory without it.

So if fear, sickness, persecution, or distressing situations come against you, always remember to TAKE COURAGE! No matter what you are going through, if it is in the world, Jesus has already overcome it. Just as His Word calmed the wind and the waves on the Sea of Galilee over two thousand years ago, Jesus' Word can calm the storm you may be facing today and impart **God's gift of peace** to your heart.

Other Books in This Series
by Cathy Duplantis

The Healing Word (Book and CD)

Other Books

How to Behave in a Cave

Keeping a Clean Heart

To contact Cathy Duplantis
write or call:

Jesse Duplantis Ministries
PO Box 1089
Destrehan, LA 70047
(985) 764-2000

Or visit us online at:
www.jdm.org

Follow Us:

*Please include your prayer requests
and praise reports when you write.*

Enhanced CD Instructions

For Windows:

1. Load the CD into your computer.

2. In Computer/My Computer, right click CD and tell it to "open."

3. The MP3 folder contains MP3 files of all 4 Steps in this book. They can be played on your computer or copied onto your tablet, phone, or other device that can play audio files.

4. The video folder contains *The Peaceful Word* MP4 video that can be played on your computer or copied onto your tablet, phone, or other device that can play videos.

For Mac:

1. Load CD into your computer.

2. On the desktop, an "Audio CD" and a "CD" icon will appear.

3. Right click the CD (not the "Audio CD") and tell it to "open."

4. The MP3 folder contains MP3 files of all 4 Steps in this book. They can be played on your computer or copied onto your tablet, phone, or other device that can play audio files.

5. The video folder contains *The Peaceful Word* MP4 video that can be played on your computer or copied onto your tablet, phone, or other device that can play videos.